THE JOY OF CHRISTMAS

"For unto us a child is born, unto us a son is given: and the government shall be upon his shoulder: and his name shall be called Wonderful, Counsellor, The mighty God, The everlasting Father, The Prince of Peace."

Isaiah 9:6

By
Franklin N. Abazie

The Joy of Christmas

COPYRIGHT 2018 BY Franklin N Abazie
ISBN: 978:1-945-133-8-55
All right reserved. This book or any portion thereof may not be reproduced or used in any manner whatsoever without the express written permission of the publisher, except for the use of brief quotations in a book review. All Bible quotes are from King James Version and others as noted.

Published by: F N ABAZIE PUBLISHING HOUSE---a.k.a,
Empowerment Bookstore:

That I may publish with the voice of thanksgiving and tell of all thy wondrous works. **Psalms26:7**

To order additional copies, wholesales or booking: Call the Church office (973-372-7518)
or Empowerment Bookstore Hotline 973-393-8518
Worship address:
343 Sanford Avenue Newark New Jersey 07106
Administrative Head Office address:
33 Schley Street Newark New Jersey 07112
Email:pastorfranknto@yahoo.com
Website www.fnabaziehealingministries.org
Publishing House: www.fnabaziepublishinghouse.org

This book is a production of F N Abazie Publishing House.

A publication Arms of Miracle of God Ministries 2018
First Edition

CONTENTS

THE MANDATE OF THE COMMISSION...........iv

ARMS OF THE COMMISSION............................v

INTRODUCTION...viii

CHAPTER 1

1. The Power of a Gift...42

CHAPTER 2

2. What is the Joy of Christmas Season?................49

CHAPTER 3

3. Prayer of Salvation...73

CHAPTER 4

4. About the Author..83

THE MANDATE OF THE COMMISSION

"THE MOMENT IS DUE TO IMPACT YOUR WORLD THROUGH THE REVIVAL OF THE HEALING & MIRACLE MINISTRY OF JESUS CHRIST OF NAZARETH.

I AM SENDING YOU TO RESTORE HEALTH UNTO THEE AND I WILL HEAL THEE OF THY WOUNDS, SAID THE LORD OF HOST."

ARMS OF THE COMMISSION

1) F N Abazie Ministries-Miracle of God Ministries (Miracle Chapel Intl)

2) F N Abazie TV Ministries: Global Television Ministry Outreach.

3) F N Abazie Radio Ministries: Radio Broadcasting Outreach.

4) F N Abazie Publishing House: Book Publication.

5) F N Abazie Bible School: also called Word of Healing Bible School (W.O.H.B.S)

6) F N Abazie Evangelistic Ass: Miracle of God Ministries: Global Crusade

7) Empowerment Bookstore: Book distribution.

8) F N Abazie Helping Hands: Meeting the help of the needy world wide

9) F N Abazie Disaster Recovery Mission: Global Disaster Recovery.

10) F N Abazie Prison Ministry: Prison Ministry for all convicts "Second chance"

Some of our ministry arms are waiting the appointed time to commence

FAVOR CONFESSION

Father thank you for making me righteous and accepted through the blood of Jesus Christ. Because of that, I am blessed and highly favored by God. I am the subject of your affection. Your favor surrounds me as a shield, and the first thing that people see around me is your favored shield.

Thank you that I have favor with you and man today. All day long people go out of their way to bless me and help me. I have favor with everyone that I deal with today. Doors that were once closed are now opened for me. I receive preferential treatment, and I have special privileges, I am Gods favored child.

No good thing will he withhold from me. Because of Gods favor my enemies cannot triumph over my life. I have supernatural increase and promotion. I declare restoration to everything that the devil has stolen from my life. I have honor in the midst of my adversaries and an increase in assets, especially in real estate and expansion of territories.

Because I am highly favored by God, I experience great victories, supernatural turnarounds, and miraculous breakthrough in the midst of great impossibilities. I receive recognition, prominence, and honor. Petitions are granted to me even by ungodly authorities. Policies, rules, regulations, and laws are changed and reverse on my behalf.

I win battles that I don't even have to fight, because God fights them for me. This is the day, the set time and the designated moment for me to experience the free favor of God, that profusely and lavishly abound on my behalf in Jesus name. Amen.

INTRODUCTION

"And this shall be a sign unto you; Ye shall find the babe wrapped in swaddling clothes, lying in a manger." **Luke2:12**

Every year millions of people gather all over the world to celebrate The Christmas holiday season. To me, it is the best part of the year; simply because, we have come to the end of another year alive. We are told, *"Thou crownest the year with thy goodness; and thy paths drop fatness."* **Psalms65:11**

Christmas season is a time when families, friends, and co-workers, get together to celebrate the end of the year, and most importantly to celebrate the birth of Jesus.

Christmas is a season that we honor the birth of Jesus Christ. The truth is, over two billion Christians embrace this season with joy and solicitude. It is supposed to be a time of joy, peace, and sharing love with everyone around us. No man or woman should be left out in this season. No one should be miserable during this season.

Christmas is a time for family and friends to get together, celebrate and exchange gifts.

The Joy of Christmas is a small book that reminds us of the Joy of the season. If you have been sad all through the year, at least, you are alive. Be happy!

"For unto us a child is born, unto us a son is given: and the government shall be upon his shoulder: and his name shall be called Wonderful, Counsellor, The mighty God, The everlasting Father, The Prince of Peace."

Christmas is a yearly birthday party, organized by Christians all over the world, to commemorate the birth of Jesus Christ.

Ironically, at most Christmas parties the person whose birthday we're supposed to be celebrating is completely ignored. He is not even mentioned. Although Jesus is the reason for the season, he's often ignored. This small book, is a reminder. May I repeat again that Jesus is the reason for the season.

Happy Reading

HIS DESTINY WAS THE CROSS….

HIS PURPOSE WAS LOVE…..

HIS REASON WAS YOU….

"In everything give thanks: for this is the will of God in Christ Jesus concerning you."

1theo5:18

"Glory to God in the highest, and on Earth, peace and goodwill towards men."

Luke 2:14

"When they saw the star they rejoiced with great joy."

Matthew 2:10

We Wish You A Merry Christmas

We wish you a merry Christmas
We wish you a Merry Christmas
We wish you a Merry Christmas
We wish you a Merry Christmas and a Happy
New Year

Good tidings we bring to you and your kin
We wish you a Merry Christmas and a Happy
New Year

Now bring us some figgy pudding
Now bring us some figgy pudding
Now bring some out here

Good tidings we bring to you and your kin
We wish you a Merry Christmas and a Happy
new Year

We won't go until we get some
We won't go until we get some
We won't go until we get some, so bring some
out here

Good tidings we bring to you and your kin
We wish you a Merry Christmas and a Happy
New Year

We wish you a Merry Christmas
We wish you a Merry Christmas
We wish you a Merry Christmas and a Happy
New Year

"And she gave birth to a son, a male child, who is to rule all the nations with a rod of iron; and her child was caught up to God and to His throne."

Rev12:5

"For a child will be born to us, a son will be given to us; And the government will rest on His shoulders; And His name will be called Wonderful Counselor, Mighty God, Eternal Father, Prince of Peace."

Isaiah9:6

"For God so loved the world, that He gave His only begotten Son, that whoever believes in Him shall not perish, but have eternal life."

John3:16

"Therefore the Lord Himself will give you a sign: Behold, a virgin will be with child and bear a son, and she will call His name Immanuel."

Isaiah 7:14

"And suddenly there appeared with the angel a multitude of the heavenly host praising God and saying, "Glory to God in the highest, And on earth peace among men with whom He is pleased"

Luke2:13-14

"Therefore no one is to act as your judge in regard to food or drink or in respect to a festival or a new moon or a Sabbath day"

Col2:16

"But as for you, Bethlehem Ephrathah, Too little to be among the clans of Judah, From you One will go forth for Me to be ruler in Israel His goings forth are from long ago, From the days of eternity."

Micah5:2

"When they saw the star, they rejoiced exceedingly with great joy."

Mathew2:10

"She will bear a Son; and you shall call His name Jesus, for He will save His people from their sins."

Mathew1:21

"When the angels had gone away from them into heaven, the shepherds began saying to one another, "Let us go straight to Bethlehem then, and see this thing that has happened which the Lord has made known to us." So they came in a hurry and found their way to Mary and Joseph, and the baby as He lay in the manger."

Luke2:15-16

"The angel answered and said to her, "The Holy Spirit will come upon you, and the power of the Most High will overshadow you; and for that reason the holy Child shall be called the Son of God."

Luke1:35

"But when the fullness of the time came, God sent forth His Son, born of a woman, born under the Law, so that He might redeem those who were under the Law, that we might receive the adoption as sons."

Gal4:4-5

"Oh give thanks to the LORD, for He is good, For His lovingkindness is everlasting."

Psalms107:1

"And she gave birth to her firstborn son; and she wrapped Him in cloths, and laid Him in a manger, because there was no room for them in the inn."

Luke2:7

"You will have joy and gladness, and many will rejoice at his birth."

Luke1:14

"Then a shoot will spring from the stem of Jesse, And a branch from his roots will bear fruit."

Isaiah11:1

"For the wages of sin is death, but the free gift of God is eternal life in Christ Jesus our Lord."

Romans6:23

"Every good thing given and every perfect gift is from above, coming down from the Father of lights, with whom there is no variation or shifting shadow."

James1:17

"Peace I leave with you; My peace I give to you; not as the world gives do I give to you Do not let your heart be troubled, nor let it be fearful."

John 14:27

"In the same region there were some shepherds staying out in the fields and keeping watch over their flock by night."

Luke2:8

"Where is He who has been born King of the Jews? For we saw His star in the east and have come to worship Him."

Mathew2:2

"Jesus, knowing that the Father had given all things into His hands, and that He had come forth from God and was going back to God."

John13:3

"And let all kings bow down before him, All nations serve him."

Psalms 72:11

"These things I have spoken to you, so that in Me you may have peace In the world you have tribulation, but take courage; I have overcome the world."

John 16:33

"After coming into the house they saw the Child with Mary His mother; and they fell to the ground and worshiped Him. Then, opening their treasures, they presented to Him gifts of gold, frankincense, and myrrh."

Mathew2:11

"And the Word became flesh, and dwelt among us, and we saw His glory, glory as of the only begotten from the Father, full of grace and truth."

John 1:14

CELEBRATE JESUS AND ENJOY THE SEASON OF CHRISTMAS

Christmas season is a great season of joy. I encourage you to enjoy this season with joy, peace, and love. If it is in your capacity, give a gift to your love ones, your friends, families, your church, and your Pastor.

Although you may all not agree with me, in my opinion, this is a season of thanksgiving. Be thankful to God. If not for any other reason, be happy that you are alive to witness the end of yet another year.

We are told…

"With long life will I satisfy him, and shew him my salvation." **Psalms91:16**.

"Thou crownest the year with thy goodness; and thy paths drop fatness." **Psalms65:11**

"But we all, with open face beholding as in a glass the glory of the Lord, are changed into the same image from glory to glory, even as by the Spirit of the Lord." **2cor3:18**

CHAPTER 1
THE POWER OF A GIFT

"A man's gift maketh room for him, and bringeth him before great men." **Proverb18:16**

"And thou shalt take no gift: for the gift blindeth the wise, and perverteth the words of the righteous." **Exodus23:8**

"...neither take a gift: for a gift doth blind the eyes of the wise, and pervert the words of the righteous." **Deut16:19**

Every gift is a seed. Whether you are receiving or giving there is power behind every gift. The season of Christmas is a season of joy, peace, and love. The love of Jesus is demonstrated by the gift you give, and the gift you recieve in love. No one should be left out in this season. *Surprisingly, even the stingiest people find joy in giving and receiving a gift during Christmas.*

It is alright to give someone a gift. It is a biblical practice to give someone a gift. Giving is an affirmation of our love in Christ Jesus. Our motives should be in love, to celebrate the Joy of the Christmas season. You are not giving because you have a negative plan ahead.

We are told, *"...neither take a gift: for a gift doth blind the eyes of the wise, and pervert the words of the righteous."* **Deut16:19**.

GIVE RIGHTEOUSLY

The golden rule ----You do not give someone what you will not like to receive. **Treat others as you will love them to treat you.**

It is written, *"And if ye offer the blind for sacrifice, is it not evil? and if ye offer the lame and sick, is it not evil? offer it now unto thy governor; will he be pleased with thee, or accept thy person? saith the Lord of hosts."* **Mal1:8**

Chapter 1 - The Power of a Gift

OUR MOTIVE TO GIVE MUST BE PURE

We are told, *"Therefore if thou bring thy gift to the altar, and there rememberest that thy brother hath ought against thee; Leave there thy gift before the altar, and go thy way; first be reconciled to thy brother, and then come and offer thy gift."* **Mathew5:23-24**

If you love The Lord Jesus, you must give, especially during Christmas season. A lot people only talk the talk, They do not take action. Please do not promise and fail people all the time. Let your word be yes or no. Listen anything besides yes and no is from the devil.

We were told withhold not good to whom it is due, when it is in your power to do it. **proverb3:27.**

"Wherefore the Lord said, Forasmuch as this people draw near me with their mouth, and with their lips do honour me, but have removed their heart far from me, and their fear toward me is taught by the precept of men:" **Isaiah29:13**

Give thanks to God in Christmas season because He kept you alive. Learn to appreciate the season of Christmas. Celebrate it with joy, peace, and love.

Genuine thanksgiving is confirmed by our giving to God: to our love ones and to our fellow brethren's. *"For God so loved the world, that he gave his only begotten Son, that whosoever believeth in him should not perish, but have everlasting life."* **John3:16**

True sacrificial giving is proven in love. *"And Solomon loved the Lord, walking in the statutes of David his father: only he sacrificed and burnt incense in high places."* **1King3:3**

God searches our heart. *"And ye shall seek me, and find me, when ye shall search for me with all your heart."* **Jer29:13**

There are a lot of orphans and less privilege people in town, reach out to them, reach out to the destitute, the widows, the drug recovering addicts, and the poor.

Chapter 1 - The Power of a Gift

The year has ended well---Thank God for it by giving a gift to someone less privilege and someone special to you.

If you really want to receive good gift, do not fake your own giving. It is written, *"Give, and it shall be given unto you; good measure, pressed down, and shaken together, and running over, shall men give into your bosom. For with the same measure that ye mete withal it shall be measured to you again."* **Luke6:38**

"If ye then, being evil, know how to give good gifts unto your children, how much more shall your Father which is in heaven give good things to them that ask him?" **Mathew7:11**

Every time you are depressed, you are living in the past, whenever you are anxious you are living in the future. But when you are at peace. You are living in the present.

I encourage you to make it a lifestyle to give good gift to people around your life every season of the year. That is--give a gift not only in Christmas season. *"Every good gift and every perfect gift is from above, and cometh down from the Father of lights, with whom is no variableness, neither shadow of turning."* **James1:17**

"O give thanks unto the Lord; for he is good: for his mercy endureth for ever." **Psalms136:1**

"O give thanks unto the God of gods: for his mercy endureth for ever." **Psalms136:2**

"O give thanks to the Lord of lords: for his mercy endureth for ever." **Psalms136:3**

"O give thanks unto the Lord, for he is good: for his mercy endureth for ever." **Psalms107:1**

"Let the redeemed of the Lord say so, whom he hath redeemed from the hand of the enemy;" **Psalms107:2**

"It is a good thing to give thanks unto the Lord, and to sing praises unto thy name, O Most High:" **Psalms 92:1**

"To shew forth thy lovingkindness in the morning, and thy faithfulness every night." **Psalms 92:2**

CHAPTER 2
WHAT IS THE JOY OF CHRISTMAS SEASON?

And the angel said unto them, Fear not: for, behold, I bring you good tidings of great joy, which shall be to all people. **Luke2:10**

The Joy of the Christmas season is to put a smile on the face of someone else. As you do; God will use someone else to put a smile on your own face. We must embrace the attitude of making ourselves happy and others happy. *"A merry heart doeth good like a medicine: but a broken spirit drieth the bones."* **Proverb17:22**

The happier you look, the happier someone will contaminate your joy. *"The spirit of a man will sustain his infirmity; but a wounded spirit who can bear?"* **Proverb18:14**

My point is, we must go out of our way to give a Christmas gift to someone in this season. That is the joy of Christmas season in a nut shell. *"A gift is as a precious stone in the eyes of him that hath it: whithersoever it turneth, it prospereth."* **Proverb17:8**

"Thou wilt shew me the path of life: in thy presence is fulness of joy; at thy right hand there are pleasures for evermore." **Psalms16:11**

The secret to enjoy this season is to put a smile on the face of someone. *"The liberal soul shall be made fat: and he that watereth shall be watered also himself."* **Proverb11:24**

Christmas season is very a significant season for the people of United States and people around the world at large. It is in commemoration of the birth of Jesus Christ of Nazareth.

Christmas day is celebrated on the 25th of December every year. Although the whole idea has been expanded to a family reunion, end of the year party, and a brief winter vacation, nevertheless, the primary reason for Christmas Holiday is to honor the birth of Jesus Christ.

Chapter 2 - What is the Joy of Christmas Season?

Immediately after Thanksgiving in November people get into the celebratory mode in anticipation for the Christmas holidays. Right after Thanksgiving Holiday, Christmas trees are erected in front of homes and offices, street decorations in full swing with Christmas trees and lights all over.

As a result of street decoration, Christmas light, and trees, everyone accepts and welcome the season of Christmas. Shopping malls, and other shopping outlets are at their highest sales give away. This makes Christmas gift affordable for everyone.

How it is Celebrated?

People in United States celebrate Christmas in a number of ways and start with the preparations much before the day arrives. Weeks before, they start with decorating their homes with bright lights, Christmas trees and other decoration items available for Christmas day.

Also, it is common that, people organize for gigantic meals with their friends and family. Various delicious dishes are prepared especially on Christmas day.

Children receive a plenty of gifts from family members and from Santa Clause. As a result, in United States, the day has become a commercialized celebration, as families incessantly spend for buying winning gifts for the children of the family and also other members of family.

Churches and schools organize events wherein, the neighborhood is decorated with a lot of gusto and enthusiasm. Also, most of the malls start erecting Christmas trees and organizing dance and other competitions.

Award winning Christmas songs played anywhere around this time attracts even pedestrians passing by. A lot of charitable organizations and individuals organize for a meal session for the children.

Chapter 2 - What is the Joy of Christmas Season?

The Special Celebration

The country celebrates the day retaining the original meaning of Christmas which goes to the service of people. It celebrates the birth of Jesus Christ! Many of the traditions adopted by United States have come from the pre-Christian winter celebrations. Some of these special and significant ways of celebration includes the decorations made with evergreen plants and with candles.

During the time of the Romans this festival of winter was celebrated when people used to organize get together with family and friends. It used to be a relaxing time for the Romans. Also, people exchanged gifts with each other and presented gifts like dolls to children. And, this festival was celebrated with the coming of the winter solstice and was celebrated on 25th December. And, the Christmas day celebration in United States has a great influence from this festival which was celebrated during the times of Romans.

Although the holiday- Christmas season is a wonderful time to celebrate with family and friends. It must become a daily ritual for us as believers. By this I mean a way of life. Appreciate God an those God planted around your life.

In this season spend time with God It is written *"Be careful for nothing; but in everything by prayer and supplication with thanksgiving let your requests be made known unto God."* **Phil4:6**

Paul and Silas took advantage of giving thanks in their prayers. It is written *"And at midnight Paul and Silas prayed, and sang praises unto God: and the prisoners heard them."* **Acts16:25**

Our faith and trust automatically will grow if we develop a lifestyle of liberality. Learn to give without expecting something in return from whom you gave.

Chapter 2 - What is the Joy of Christmas Season?

Prayer 1: A Daily Thanksgiving Prayer

"Dear God, Thank you for your awesome power and work in our lives, thank you for your greatness and for your blessings over us. Thank you for your great love and care. Thank you for your sacrifice so that we might have freedom and life. Forgive us for when we don't thank you enough. Amen"

Prayer 2: A Prayer for a Thankful Heart

"Lord Jesus, Instruct me to offer you a heart of thanksgiving and praise in all my daily experiences of life. Teach me to be joyful always, to pray continually, and to give thanks in all my circumstances. I accept them as your will for my life. Amen"

Prayer 3: A Prayer of Thanks

"Father I thank you for my life, family, and love ones, oftentimes life challenges pull me down and I find difficult to give you thanks. Open my heart to recognize all the good things you have done so far in my life. I thank you Jesus for my life. Amen."

Prayer 4: A Prayer to Teach children to be Thankfulness

"Lord Jesus, I pray that you will put it in the heart of every child to be thankful in life. Father give them a purpose and let your joy become their strength. I thank you for all you have done in our lives. Amen"

Prayer 5: A Thanksgiving Day Prayer

"Our Heavenly Father:

We thank Thee for food and remember the hungry.

We thank Thee for health and remember the sick.

We thank Thee for friends and remember the friendless.

We thank Thee for freedom and remember the enslaved.

May these remembrances stir us to service. That Thy gifts to us may be used for others. Amen."

Chapter 2 - What is the Joy of Christmas Season?

Prayer 6: Confession of Gratitude

"Thank you, God for the times You have said "no." They have helped me depend on You so much more.

Thank you, God, for unanswered prayer. It reminds me that You know what's best for me, even when my opinion differs from Yours.

Thank You, Lord, for the things you have withheld from me. You have protected me from what I may never realize.

Thank You Jesus, for the doors You have closed in my life. And for the present open door in my life. Lord let your will be done in my life. Amen

Thank you, Jesus for food on my table daily.

Thank you, Lord, for the alone times in my life. Those times have forced me to lean in closer to You.

Thank you, God, for the uncertainties I've experienced. They have deepened my trust in You.

The Joy of Christmas by Franklin N. Abazie

Thank You, Lord, for the times You came through for me when I didn't even know I needed a rescue.

Thank You, Lord, for the losses I have experienced. They have been a reminder that You are my greatest gain.

Thank You, God, for the tears I have shed.

They have kept my heart soft and mold-able.

Thank You, God, for the times I haven't been able to control my circumstances. They have reminded me that You are sovereign and on the throne.

Thank You, God, for the life of every living person you planted somehow into my life. I give you praise for what you have done and for what you are doing in my life.

Thank You, God that I have an inheritance in the heavenly places...I desire to be with you one day in eternity. Amen

Thank You, God, for the greatest gift You could ever give me: forgiveness through Your perfect Son's death on the cross on my behalf.

Chapter 2 - What is the Joy of Christmas Season?

Thank You, God, for the righteousness You credited toward me, through the death and resurrection of Jesus. It's a righteousness I could never earn or attain on my own.

Thank You, Father, that You know me, You hear me, and You see my tears. Remind me through difficult times that You are my God, You are on the throne, and You are eternally good.

And thank You, Lord, not only for my eternal salvation, but for the salvation You afford every day of my life as You save me from myself, my foolishness, my own limited insights, and my frailties in light of Your power and strength."

CONCLUSION

"And this shall be a sign unto you; Ye shall find the babe wrapped in swaddling clothes, lying in a manger." **Luke2:12**

Christmas season is a great time to fellowship with God.I encourage you to develop a quality relationship with the Holy Spirit.

Don't enter the new year with the old miserable, defeated spirit.Jesus is Lord.

"Therefore if any man be in Christ, he is a new creature: old things are passed away; behold, all things are become new." **2cor5:17**

Now repeat this Prayer after me

Say Lord Jesus, I accept you today, as my Lord and my savior, forgive me of my sins wash me with your blood. Right now, I believe, I am sanctified, I am save, I am free, I am free from the Power of sin to serve the Lord Jesus. Thank you Lord for saving me. Amen.

Chapter 2 - What is the Joy of Christmas Season?

What must I do to determine my divine visitation?

To determine divine visitation you must be born again. The word says as many as received him, to them gave He power to become the sons of God. Even to them that believe on his name.

To qualify for divine visitation do the following sincerely;

1) Acknowledge that you are a sinner and that He died for you. **Rom3:23**.

2) Repent of your sins. **Acts 3:19, Luke13:5, 2Peter3:9**

3) Believe in your heart that Jesus died for your sin. **Romans10:10**

4) Confess Jesus as the Lord over your life. **Romans10:10, Acts2:21**

Now repeat this Prayer after me

Say Lord Jesus, I accept you today, as my Lord and my savior, forgive me of my sins wash me with your blood. Right now, I believe, I am sanctified, I am save, I am free, I am free from the Power of sin to serve the Lord Jesus. Thank you Lord for saving me.

I adjure you to watch the Spirit of God bear witness with your Spirit confirming His word with signs following. The word says The Spirit itself beareth witness with our spirit, that we are the children of God.

Join a bible believing church or join us on our weekly and Sunday worship services at 343 Sanford Avenue Newark New Jersey 07106.

Chapter 2 - What is the Joy of Christmas Season?

WISDOM KEYS

Every Productive Society is a society heading to the top

Millions of Nigerians run away from Nigeria, very few Nigerians stay in Nigeria.

My decision to return Nigeria is the will of God for my life

My short coming in America after 18 years, trained me to be wise, to think, reflect and reason appropriately.

If you train your mind to reason it will train your hands to earn money.

It is absurd to use the money of the heathen to build the kingdom of the living God.

Every Ministry reveals its agenda and goal either at the beginning or at the end. Be careful of your life it is your first Ministry.

The average American mind is conditioned for a continual quest to get new things and (discard the former) and throw away old things.

When I considered well, my BMW jeep became my initial deposit for the work of the ministry in Nigeria

Everyone is waiting for you to change your mind until you change your thinking nothing changes around you.

Multiple academic degrees in other discipline gave me the chance to think, reflect and reason

What so everyone are thinking and reflecting at the moment reveals you to the time and the now factor

All events and intents are the product of precise thought processes, accurate reason every event is designed for a designated timeline

Wisdom is your ability to think, to create and invent. If you can think wise enough you will come out of penury

The distance between you and success is your creative ability to think reason and reflect accurate.

Chapter 2 - What is the Joy of Christmas Season?

Success is the result of hard work, commitment resolve and determination learning from past mistakes and failing.

If you organize your mind you have organized your life and destiny.

There is a thin line between success and failure. If you look above and beyond you are on your way to success.

Wealth is your ability to think, power is your ability to reason and success is your ability to be informed.

If you can make use of your mind by thinking and reasoning God will make use of your life and destiny.

Think and Be Great

Reflect, Reason, think and be great

Famous people are born of woman

That you will make it is your intention; that you will survive is your resolve, that you will succeed with changes is your determination, personal efforts and hard work.

No man was born a failure. Lack of vision is the end product of failure.

Working with mental patients encourages and aspire me to be a productive observant and dedicated to my assignment.

Successful people are not magicians, it is the will power combined with hard work, and determination and a resolve to succeed that make them succeed.

In the unequivocal state of the mind, intention is not a location or a position it is the state of the mind.

So many people think that they think. The mind is used to think reflect and reason. You will remain blind with your eye open until you can see with your mind by thinking.

There is no favoritism in accurate and precise calculation

Chapter 2 - What is the Joy of Christmas Season?

Although knowledge is power, information is the key and gateway to a great future.

It will take the hand of God to move the hand of man.

With the backing of the great wise God, nothing will disconnect you from your inheritance.

As long as you have wisdom and understanding of God, Satan and evil cannot manipulate your life and destiny.

You have come this far by yourself judgment and decision you have made in the past, now lean and listen to God for another dimension of greatness.

Great people are common people it is extra ordinary effort and the price of sacrifice that produces greatness.

As a mental direct care worker I saw a great pastor and a motivational speaker within myself.

Menial job does not reduce your self-worth, until you resolve to achieve greatness see greatness in all you do; you will never count in your community

The principle of Jesus will solve your gambling and addiction problems

The man of Jesus will lead you into heaven,

Everyone have their self-appraisal and what they think about you. Until you discover yourself other opinion about you will alter the real you.

Supervisors and directors are just a position in the chain of command in a work place. Never allow your supervisor hierarchy to alter your opinion about yourself.

Everyone can come out of debt if they make up their mind.

That I am not a decision maker at work does not diminish my contribution to my world.

Although it appears like it was a poor decision to accept a direct care employment at a psychiatric hospital as I reflect of my nine years of experience, it became apparent that I have learnt and experienced enough for my next assignment.

Self-encouragement and determination is a resolve of the heart.

Chapter 2 - What is the Joy of Christmas Season?

If you are determined to make a difference, and do the things that make a difference you will eventually make a difference.

Good things do not come easy

Short cuts will cut your life short.

Those who look ahead move ahead.

Life is all about making an impact. In your life time strive to make an impact in your community.

Make friends and connect with people who are moving ahead of you in life.

If you can look around well you have come a long way in your life, made a lot of difference and realized a lot of success in life.

If you are my old friend, hurry up to reach out to me before I become a stranger to you.

Everything I am blessed with inspirations from God, that change my definition and interpretation of the world around me.

I thought I was stagnant and lonely until I looked around and noticed my children running around and my wife cooking.

The Joy of Christmas by Franklin N. Abazie

At 40 I resigned my Job to seek the Lord forever.

My ministry took a drastic rise to the top when the wisdom of God visited me with knowledge and understanding.

You will be a better person if you understand the characteristics of your personality – your mood swings attitudes and habits.

It is the seed of love you sow into the heart of a child and a woman that you reap in due time.

Love is not selfish, love share everything including the concealed secrets of the mind.

As long as you have a prayer life and a bible; you will never feel lonely, rejected and idle in the race of life.

When good friends disconnect from you, let them go, they might have seen something new in a different direction.

Confidence in yourself and in God is the only way to bring you out of captivity

Never train a child to waste his/her time.

The mind is the greatest assets of a great future.

Chapter 2 - What is the Joy of Christmas Season?

You walk by common sense run by principles and fly by instruction.

Those who fly in flight of life fly alone.

Up in the air you are alone. No one can toll you accept the compass of knowledge and information

I have seen a tolling vehicle I have seen a tolling ship I have never seen a tolling airplane.

I exercise my judgment and make a decision every minute of the day.

Decisions are crucial, critical and vital with reference to your future.

So many people wish for a great future. You can only work towards a great future.

Your celebrity status began when you discovered your talent. What are you good at? Work at it with all commitment.

Prayers will sustain you but the wisdom of God will prosper you.

When I met Oyedepo, his teachings changed my perspective, but when I met Ibiyeomie; His teaching changed my perception.

I will be successful in ministry if only I concentrate and focus my energy in the work of the ministry.

It took the late Dr. Vincent Pearle Norman's book to open my mind towards kingdom success.

CHAPTER 3
PRAYER OF SALVATION

"Neither is there salvation in any other: for there is none other name under heaven given among men, whereby we must be saved." **Acts4:12**

There is only one name that will take us all into heaven.

What must I do to determine my salvation?

To be saved we must be born again!

The word says as many as received him, to them gave He power to become the sons of God. Even to them that believe on his name.

To qualify for divine visitation do the following sincerely,

1) Acknowledge that you are a sinner and that He died for you. **Rom3:23.**

2) Repent of your sins. **Acts 3:19, Luke13:5, 2Peter3:9**

3) Believe in your heart that Jesus died for your sin. **Romans10:10**

4) Confess Jesus as the Lord over your life. **Romans10:10, Acts2:21**

Now repeat this Prayer after me

Say Lord Jesus, I accept you today, as my Lord and my savior, forgive me of my sins wash me with your blood. Right now, I believe, I am sanctified, I am save, I am free, I am free from the Power of sin to serve the Lord Jesus. Thank you Lord for saving me. Amen.

I adjure you to watch the Spirit of God bear witness with your Spirit confirming His word with signs following. The word says The Spirit itself beareth witness with our spirit, that we are the children of God.

Chapter 3 - Prayer of Salvation

MIRACLE CARE OUTREACH

"...But that the members should have the same care one for another" **1cor12:25**

We are all members of the body of Christ. Jesus commanded us to love our neighbor as ourselves. This includes caring for one another as a member of one body. True love is expressed in caring and giving. The word says for God so Love He gave....

Reach out to someone in need of Jesus, help someone in crisis find Christ. Look out and prove your love to Jesus by caring and inviting your friends and associates to find Jesus the Healer.

Invite your friends to our Home Care Cell Fellowship (Miracle chapel Intl Satellite fellowship) In the USA at 33 Schley Street Newark New Jersey 07112.

If you are in Nigeria—**MIRACLE OF GOD MINISTRIES**

A.K.A"MIRACLE CHAPEL INTL"
Mpama –Egbu-Owerri Imo state Nigeria.

(Home Care Cell fellowship Group).We meet every Tuesday at 6:00pm-7:00pm.

LIFE IS NOT ALL ABOUT DURATION BUT ITS ALL ABOUT DONATION

What does the above statement mean?....

"Life consists not in accumulation of material wealth.." **Luke12:15.**

"But it's all about liberality….meaning-what you can give and share with others." **Proverb11:25.**

When you live for others--You live forever- because you out live your generation by the legacy you live behind after you depart into glory to be with the Lord. But when you live to yourself - you are reduced to self—you are easily forgotten when you die and depart in glory.

Permit me to admonish you today to live your life to be a blessing to a soul connected to you today.

Chapter 3 - Prayer of Salvation

I want you to know that so many souls are connected and looking up to you, and through you so many souls will be saved and rescued from destruction. Will you disciple someone today to find Jesus Christ?

"As a genuine Christian; it is your duty to evangelize Jesus Christ to all you meet on your way. Jesus is still in the healing business-Jesus is still doing miracles from time of old to now.

Therefore tell someone about Jesus Christ today, disciple and bring them to Church."

John 1:45 Philip findeth Nathanael....

Please to prove the sincerity of your love for God today; please become a soul winner. The dignity of your Christianity is hidden in your boldness to proclaim and evangelize Jesus Christ to all you meet on your way.

There is a question mark on the integrity of your Christianity until you become a life soul winner. Invite someone to join us worship the Lord Jesus this coming Sunday.

MIRACLE OF GOD MINISTRIES

PILLARS OF THE COMMISSION

We Believe Preach and Practice the following,

1) We believe and preach Salvation to every living human being

2) We believe and preach Repentance and forgiveness of sins

3) We believe and preach the baptism of the Holy Spirit and Spiritual gifts

4) We believe and teach the Prosperity

5) We believe and preach Divine Healing and Miracles (Signs & Wonder)

6) We believe and preach Faith

7) We believe and Proclaim the Power of God (Supernatural)

8) We believe and Proclaim Praise & Worship to God

Chapter 3 - Prayer of Salvation

9) We believe and preach Wisdom

10) We believe and preach Holiness (Consecration)

11) We believe and preach Vision

12) We believe and teach the Word of God

13) We believe and teach Success

14) We believe and practice Prayer

15) We believe and teach Deliverance

This 15 stones form the Pillars of Our Commission.

Become part of this church family and follow this great move of God.

MY HEART FELT PRAYER FOR YOU

Lord, I long for your joy during this Christmas season. Protect me and my family during this season. Let us safely into the new year. In Jesus Mighty Name. Amen

The Joy of Christmas by Franklin N. Abazie

Now let me Pray for you:

Father Lord, give us the grace to appreciate all your goodness, kindness, love, upon our lives. Lord, keep us alive to see another new year in Jesus Mighty Name. **Amen.**

WORSHIP CENTER

MIRACLE OF GOD MINISTRIES INC

343 SANFORD AVENUE NEWARK NEW JERSEY 07106

WWW.FNABAZIEHEALINGMINISTRIES.ORG

EMAIL: PASTORFRANKNTO@YAHOO.COM

CHURCH HEAD OFFICE TEL:973-372-7518

PASTOR CELL 973-393-8518

PRAYERLINE: 515-739-1216 CODE 168822

WEDNESDAYS ONLY 9:00PM EASTERN TIME ---10:00PM EASTERN TIME

Chapter 3 - Prayer of Salvation

It is my prayer that you find time to reach out to us as a ministry. If you need prayer we are here to help you. Some of my sermons and other material will be helpful to your spiritual life.

The Lord Richly be with you Amen.

WHAT DO I DO THEN , IN THIS SEASON:

BE HAPPY

It is written,

"A merry heart doeth good like a medicine: but a broken spirit drieth the bones." **Proverb17:22**

"The spirit of a man will sustain his infirmity; but a wounded spirit who can bear?" **Proverb18:14**

BE JOYFUL

"...neither be ye sorry; for the joy of the Lord is your strength." **Neh8:10**

"Whom having not seen, ye love; in whom, though now ye see him not, yet believing, ye rejoice with joy unspeakable and full of glory:" **1Peter1:8.**

BE EXICITED

No one is responsible to keep you excited and inspired. May the Holy Spirit help you remain inspired and excited during Christmas season.

Amen

CHAPTER 4
ABOUT THE AUTHOR

Rev Franklin N Abazie is the founding and Presiding Pastor of Miracle of God Ministries with headquarters in Newark, New Jersey USA and a branch church in Owerri- Imo State Nigeria. He is following the footsteps of one of his mentors, Oral Roberts (Healing Evangelist) of the blessed memory.

The Lord passed Oral Roberts healing mantle two days before he went to be with the Lord at age 91 into the hand of healing evangelist-Rev Franklin N Abazie in a vision.

In all his services the Power and Presence of God is present to heal all in his audience. He is an ordained man of God with a Healing Ministry reviving the healing and miracle ministry of Jesus Christ of Nazareth.

Pastor Franklin N Abazie, is called by God with a unique mandate:

"THE MOMENT IS DUE TO IMPACT YOUR WORLD THROUGH THE REVIVAL OF THE HEALING & MIRACLE MINISTRY OF JESUS CHRIST OF NAZARETH.

I AM SENDING YOU TO RESTORE HEALTH UNTO THEE AND I WILL HEAL THEE OF THY WOUNDS. SAID THE LORD OF HOST"

He is a gifted ardent Teacher of the word of God who operates also in the office of a Prophet, generating and attracting undeniable signs & wonders, special miracles and healings, with apostolic fireworks of the Holy Ghost.

He is the founding and presiding senior Pastor of this fast growing Healing ministry.

He has written over 86 inspirational, healing and transforming books covering almost all aspect of divine healing and life. He is happily married and blessed with children.

BOOKS BY REV FRANKLIN N ABAZIE

1) Commanding Abundance
2) The outcome of faith
3) Understanding the secret of prevailing prayers
4) Understanding the secret of the man God uses
5) Activating my due Season
6) Overcoming Divine Verdicts
7) The Outcome of Divine Wisdom
8) Understanding God's Restoration Mandate
9) Walking in the Victory and Authority of the truth
10) Gods Covenant Exemption
11) Destiny Restoration Pillars
12) Provoking Acceptable Praise
13) Understanding Divine Judgment
14) Activating Angelic Re-enforcement
15) Provoking Un-Merited Favor
16) The Benefits of the Speaking faith
17) Understanding Divine Arrangement

18) Understanding Divine Healing
19) The Mystery of Endurance
20) Obeying Divine Instructions
21) Understanding the Voice of God
22) Never give up on Hope
23) The prevailing Power of faith
24) Understanding Divine Prosperity
25) The Reward of Prayer
26) Covenant Keys to Answered Prayers
27) Activating the Forces of Vengeance
28) Put your faith to work
29) Where is your trust?
30) The Audacity of the Blood of Jesus
31) Redeeming Your Days
32) The force of Vision
33) Breaking the shackles of Family Curses
34) Wisdom for Marriage Stability
35) The winners Faith
36) The Prayer solution
37) The power of Prayer
38) Prayer strategy
39) The prayer that works
40) Walking in Forgiveness
41) The power of the grace of God

42) The power of Persistence
43) Overcoming Divine verdicts
44) The audacity of the blood of Jesus.
45) The prevailing power of the blood of Jesus
46) The benefit of the speaking faith.
47) Fearless faith
48) Redeeming Your Days.
49) The Supernatural Power of Prophecy
50) The companionship of the Holy Spirit
51) Understanding Divine Judgement
52) Understanding Divine Prosperity
53) Dominating Controlling Forces
54) The winners Faith
55) Destiny Restoration Pillars
56) Developing Spiritual Muscles
57) Inexplicable faith
58) The lifestyle of Prayer
59) Developing a positive attitude in life.
60) The mystery of Divine supply
61) Encounter with God's Power
62) Walking in love
63) Praying in the Spirit
64) How to provoke your testimony

65) Walking in the reality of the Anointing
66) The reality of new birth
67) The price of freedom
68) The Supernatural power of faith
69) The Power of Persistence
70) The intellectual components of Redemption
71) Overcoming Fear
72) The Force of Vision
73) Overcoming Prevailing Challenges
74) The Power of the Grace of God
75) My life & Ministry
76) The Mystery of Praise

MIRACLE OF GOD MINISTRIES

NIGERIA CRUSADE 2012

MIRACLE OF GOD MINISTRIES
NIGERIA CRUSADE 2012

**MIRACLE
OF
GOD
MINISTRIES**

NIGERIA CRUSADE

2012

MIRACLE OF GOD MINISTRIES

NIGERIA CRUSADE

2012

www.ingramcontent.com/pod-product-compliance
Lightning Source LLC
Chambersburg PA
CBHW030101100526
44591CB00008B/219